WB YEATS

First published in Great Britain in 1999 by Brockhampton Press
a member of the Hodder Headline Group
20 Bloomsbury Street, London WC1B 3QA

ISBN 1-86019-9615

A copy of the CIP data is available from the
British Library upon request.

Designed and produced for Brockhampton Press
by Keith Pointing Design Consultancy.

Reprographics by Global Colour
Printed in Singapore.

Photographs of Yeats Courtesy of Bord Failte - Irish Tourist Board

Poems published with kind permission of A.P. Watt Ltd
on behalf of Michael B. Yeats.
And Reprinted with the permission of Scribner,
a Division of Simon & Schuster from
The Collected Works of W.B. Yeats, Volume 1: The Poems.
Revised and Edited by Richard J. Finneran (New York: Scribner, 1997)

WB YEATS

A BIOGRAPHY WITH
SELECTED POEMS

ANDREW LAMBIRTH

BROCKHAMPTON PRESS
LONDON

CONTENTS

BACKGROUND AND EARLY YEARS *7*

YEATS THE POET *19*

SEARCHING FOR AN IDENTITY *35*

MATURITY *41*

PERSONAL RECOLLECTIONS *51*

LATE FLOWERING AND DEATH *61*

THE POEMS *77*

INDEX OF FIRST LINES *119*

FURTHER READING *120*

I

BACKGROUND AND EARLY YEARS

WILLIAM BUTLER YEATS was born on 13th June 1865 at Sandymount, a seaside suburb of Dublin. The Yeatses were of Yorkshire origin, who, by the end of the 17th century had settled in Dublin. The second name 'Butler' was a prestigious one, descending as it did from an 18th century marriage into the family of the Dukes of Ormonde. WB's father, John Butler Yeats (1839-1922), came from a clerical family, but showed no intention of following his father or grandfather into the Church of Ireland. He trained first as a barrister, but then decided to throw it all up and become a painter. He was by nature gregarious and easy going, and notoriously bad with money. The poet John Masefield called JB Yeats 'one of the wittiest talkers of his time'. His father, John Yeats, had been rector of Drumcliff in County Sligo, and it was there that JB met his future wife, Susan Pollexfen, who had one blue eye and one brown, and was reputed to be 'the most beautiful girl in Sligo'.

The Pollexfens were Cornish in-comers, sea-farers who had built up a very successful shipping business based in Sligo. Susan was used to a certain way of life, a certain degree of comfort, and no doubt expected her husband to continue to supply this for her. She was to be disappointed. WB Yeats' parents cannot have been outwardly more different. His father the conversationalist, happier to tell you what brilliant paintings he was about to do than to actually complete them, and his mother silent, with no interest in painting at all. It's on record that she never visited a show of her husband's work nor set foot in his studio. She apparently read very little but loved her native countryside with an abiding passion, and spent hours exchanging tales of local ghosts and fairies.

WB Yeats was a delicate boy with an olive complexion, who looked almost foreign. From the start he had bad eyesight and was later to go blind in one eye. As a child in Sligo he delighted to go out ratting or rabbiting with a couple of the farm dogs, and he said later that they may have taught him to dream. WB was the eldest son, then there was Robert, who died a child, and two daughters, Susan and Elizabeth. Their names were shortened respectively to Willie, Bobbie, Lily and Lolly. In 1871, Jack Yeats was born, who grew up to be Ireland's leading expressionist painter. It was a creative family: Lily and Lolly were to found the Cuala Press which printed beautiful limited editions of all WB's works as well as books by his friends.

GLENA MOUNTAIN

LONDON IN THE LATE NINETEENTH CENTURY

In July 1867 the family moved to London, in the wake of Yeats' father who had determined to study painting at Heatherley's Art School. They lived in Fitzroy Road, Regent's Park, but much of the time was spent back at grandfather Pollexfen's home in Sligo. (Between 1872 and 1874 the family were in Ireland full time.) Already Yeats' interests were beginning to polarize: he inherited his father's curiosity of intellect coupled with his mother's fascination for the supernatural. It was at William Pollexfen's house that Yeats overheard a servant tell his mother that she'd heard the Banshee cry for his young brother the night before the child died. And it was there that he saw his first fairy, which came to him down a moonbeam.

In 1874 the family moved to 14 Edith Villas in West Kensington, and the following year Yeats was sent to the Godolphin School at Hammersmith, which he strongly disliked. In his *Autobiographies* (1955), Yeats maintained that he was miserable as a child, though no one was specifically unkind to him. He never had a proper education, and was erratic in his spelling and punctuation. But very early on he learnt how to project a powerful image of himself which masked his inner fear and anxiety. In 1876 the Yeatses moved again, this time to Bedford Park, the first of the garden suburbs, into a distinctly arty neighbourhood. Their house in Woodstock Road had William Morris wallpaper and peacock blue woodwork.

By 1880 the Yeatses had returned to Ireland, and rented a thatched cottage on the cliffs at Howth. Yeats began assiduously to collect local stories, many of which were to reappear in his early book Celtic Twilight (1893). At this time, he was attending the Erasmus Smith High School, and would travel to Dublin with his father every morning and breakfast with him in his studio there, while the older man read poetry out loud. Yeats was a solitary boy, a dreamer, lost for much of the time in romantic reverie. On summer nights he liked to sleep in a cave, at other times he retreated to a thicket near the cliffs to think. Already he was attracted to hidden wisdom and magic power, perhaps as a compensation for his physical clumsiness. (Although he pretended to be something of an athlete, he was maladroit, and in later years would hazard his life by ignoring pavements however car-crowded the streets.) He had already started writing poetry, largely in imitation of Shelley and Edmund Spenser.

In 1883 the family moved yet again, this time to 10 Ashfield Terrace in Rathgar, another Dublin suburb. The following year Yeats left school in order to attend the Metropolitan School of Art in Kildare Street where his father taught and his sisters had gone the year before. It's revealing that he refused to go up to Trinity College, Dublin, where both his father and grand-father had gone, perhaps because he doubted his talents as a scholar. However, it was at the art school that he met George Russell, a highly gifted

FROM THE HILL, HOWTH

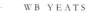

KILLINEY

student, already fast on his way to becoming a mystic. Russell was to sign himself in future as AE, letters he took from the word aeon, which came to him in a vision as the name of heavenly man. He was a far better artist than Yeats, but although he wrote a great deal throughout his life, he had less literary ability. He was a gifted seer, and altogether a remarkable man.

One of the key factors in Yeats' development as man and poet was his relationship with his father. (By comparison, his mother's direct influence upon him was negligible.) There was a lifelong tension between the two, which was only somewhat eased by the old man's departure for America in 1908, where he remained until his death. From America regular communication continued by letter. In truth Yeats feared his father. As Richard Ellmann has written, JB Yeats 'knew his son through and through, and could pierce his self-protective armour with a word.' Sometimes the quarrels and disagreements became physical. When the father discovered that aged nine his son couldn't read, he coerced and terrorized him into learning. What psychic damage did he do the boy? Perhaps WB Yeats' pursuit of supernatural knowledge was in part a recourse to an alternative power base, which could protect him from his father or even make him his equal.

Yet the relationship is by no means clear-cut. Yeats sought his father's praise and approval, and increasingly he won it. And JB Yeats' theories about art and life were to be of the utmost importance in moulding the young poet's attitude to his calling. For instance, JB Yeats believed that art should be grounded in experience, as his son was later to profess that poetic truth should spring from the soil. Also JB Yeats maintained that poetry and art were forms of truth far superior to all others. This essentially 19th century belief was carried forward by the son into the 20th century, and gave authority to his pronouncements.

In 1885 WB Yeats started the Dublin Hermetic Society. He was a great joiner and organizer, and was obviously capable of putting across his own opinions and directing the course of events. He was assertive, and at the same time strangely timid, as if in his own personality he needed to combine (though perhaps never entirely reconcile) the polar opposites. His recklessness and self-belief drove him to defy his father and abandon his study of art for poetry, but his uncertainty ensured that he continued to live at home until the October of 1895.

WOMAN CARRYING TURF

II

YEATS THE POET

In 1885 a poem of Yeats' appeared in print for the first time, in the Dublin University Review. That same year he met John O'Leary, the old Fenian leader, who was to be a seminal influence on the young man. He also met Katharine Tynan, the poet, who encouraged him to write and also took him to his first seance, at which Yeats over-reacted violently. In 1886 he decided to leave art school and concentrate on becoming a writer. Once again the family moved back to London, to Earl's Court then back to Bedford Park. In 1887 Yeats met Madame Blavatsky, the founder of the Theosophical Society. Yeats was at once struck by her powerful personality, joined the Blavatsky Lodge and began seriously to explore the mystical phenomena he was so drawn to.

That year, 1887, Yeats celebrated his first publication in England, with a poem appearing in a magazine called *The Leisure Hour*. In 1888 he published Fairy and *Folk Tales of the Irish Peasantry*. He was becoming something of an authority: in June he lectured to the Irish Literary Club of Southwark on Sligo fairies. Yeats maintained his links with Sligo, returning there whenever he could, to stay with his uncle George Pollexfen. In this house was a servant called Mary Battle, an untrained seer, full of dreams and visions which Yeats enthusiastically recorded and absorbed. (Second sight was an accepted aspect of life in those days.) These experiences were a crucial inspiration to his poetry, and in 1889 his first volume of verse appeared, entitled *The Wanderings of Oisin and Other Poems*.

Inevitably he was caught up in the mood of the times, and his early experiences were to be important for his subsequent development. He marinated in the all-pervading English fin-de-siecle romanticism, his roots spreading deep into the Aesthetic Movement of Walter Pater and Oscar Wilde. An early influence was William Morris whom he often visited at Kelmscott House on the river at Chiswick. Morris tried to help him and often invited him for dinner, where Yeats first met George Bernard Shaw. At this point, Yeats, homesick for Ireland (it was now that he wrote *The Lake Isle of Innisfree*), and uncertain of his direction, was shuttling from one mentor to another. The poet, journalist and editor WE Henley was the next, and Yeats was in future to say that it was under Henley that he really began his education. And at Henley's he first met Oscar Wilde.

IRISH COUNTRY FAIR

When Yeats met Wilde, Oscar disapproved of the colour of his shoes. Yeats was never to forget that: his carefully-constructed pose had a flaw. He was anyway somewhat shy and clumsy in such illustrious company and criticism only made things worse. It wasn't easy to break into London society, with all its rules and expectations, and Yeats would frequently bolt back to Sligo to recover his nerve. But Wilde was not unkind: in 1888, for instance, he invited Yeats to eat Christmas dinner at his Chelsea home. He also wrote that there was 'nobility of treatment and nobility of subject matter' in *The Wanderings of Oisin*. Not all reviewers were so generous.

At this stage in his career Yeats wrote pastoral poems, filled with pigs and scarecrows and fiddlers. Lord David Cecil called him 'a kind of Irish Rosetti', but went on to identify something untamed and exotic in his inspiration. Myth was there, and strange heroisms. Yeats later assumed the vague language of the Cheshire Cheese poets. In 1891 The Rhymers Club was formed by Yeats, fellow poet Ernest Rhys and the Gaelic scholar TW Rolleston. It met to read poetry in an upper room of the Cheshire Cheese pub off Fleet Street, a famous watering hole frequented in the past by the likes of Samuel Johnson and Charles Dickens. Yeats took a leading role (showing again that talent for organization - Sean O'Casey was to call him mockingly 'the Great Founder') but the enterprise was not a success.

In 1889 Yeats met Maud Gonne and was changed forever. She was remarkable to look at: six feet tall, flamboyant and said to be the most beautiful woman in Ireland. All her passion was for freeing Ireland from the English yoke; ironically in the process of imparting her enthusiasm, she enslaved Yeats, who feel deeply and romantically in love with her. She wanted him as a friend but couldn't countenance him as a lover. They saw each other a lot, and began to share heroic dreams for the future of Ireland. Although Yeats' most suitable role was to set standards for an Irish literary renaissance, he was drawn into active politics by his desire to protect and be near Maud. For her he wanted to be the hairy-chested man of action, though everything conspired against it. Perhaps it was a good thing Maud Gonne spurned Yeats' love - he might never have been able to live up to it and her. And then what would have happened to the poetry? Perhaps he began to realize this. Gradually, he dropped active political involvement to concentrate on promoting literary nationalism. In 1891 he helped to found an Irish Literary Society in London; the following year he did the same in Dublin.

Maud Gonne was also fascinated by the supernatural, and accompanied Yeats to seances. She was intensely superstitious. On the eve of a demonstration she would symbolically free caged birds such as larks and finches. Although not particularly interested in theosophy, Maud did want

MAUD GONNE

THE DEVIL'S GLEN

help with her troubled private life. Theosophy was a strange synthesis of science, religion and philosophy. When Yeats met Madame Blavatsky he had much admired her, whether she was, as many people thought, a fraud or not. She was as strong-willed as Yeats himself, and he respected that. With two such powerful personalities, there was bound to come a clash sooner or later, and in 1890 Yeats was excommunicated from the Theosophical Society for giving a lecture Blavatsky did not approve of. By then he'd had five years of access to secret and ancient wisdom with which to enrich his poetic identity, and he wished to continue his studies.

So in 1890, Yeats joined the Hermetic Order of the Golden Dawn, a similar organization to the Theosophists. Membership gave him much wider opportunities for research and experimentation with the supernatural. There was also emphasis placed upon the notion of spiritual rebirth, which Yeats, often dissatisfied with his inner self, was attracted to. He later spoke of the Order as being the chief influence on his thought before he was 40. He certainly identified with it strongly, defying the satanic Aleister Crowley, whom he thought mad and bad, and refusing to initiate him into the Order. After 1911, Yeats was increasingly interested in spiritualism, in mediums and the afterlife, and conducted his research mostly at seances.

He had a strange other-worldly appearance. In Max Beerbohm's much later cartoon, *Some Persons of the 90s*, done in 1925, Yeats' far apart wide eyes are emphasized. An early drawing of him by AE does the same. By 1896 Yeats had shaved off an early beard and dispensed also with the moustache which succeeded it, and wore black almost exclusively. Thin faced, with glowing dark eyes, he looked every inch the poet. That year he first met Lady Gregory at Tulira Castle, Edward Martyn's home in County Galway, when visiting with fellow Rhymer Arthur Symons. Her husband Sir William Gregory had died in 1889, leaving his widow with money and energy to invest in a suitable project. The specific focus of her attention became the founding of an Irish National Theatre, her larger project being WB Yeats. Augusta Gregory was an enormous influence on Yeats. She gave him a central security, a home in her house at Coole to which he could always return. Indeed he spent every summer there for 30 years, and many winters too. Coole Park was his sanity and his retreat. Lady Gregory herself gave him untold emotional support when he suffered for love of Maud Gonne. She was eminently practical too: she sent him gifts of food and wine in London and was always ready to lend him money.

In 1899 the first production of Yeats' play *The Countess Cathleen* was staged in Dublin. It caused the most fantastic brouhaha and was swiftly condemned as heretical. Yeats saw it through regardless, ensuring it was

CASTLE BY RIVER

WB YEATS EARLY 1900S AT THE ABBEY THEATRE, DUBLIN, LECTURING THE THE AUDIENCE

staged and not banned, and he was at once the hero and villain of the piece. The story is a thinly disguised homage to Ireland and Maud Gonne, and Yeats followed it up in 1902 with a one act drama *Cathleen ni Houlihan*, which this time starred Maud Gonne herself. (At one time she had entertained ideas of a theatrical career.) In 1904 the Abbey Theatre opened to increasing acclaim, and became the base for this Irish revival. The Abbey actors built up an enviable reputation for their economy of gesture and stillness on stage, a complete and refreshing contrast to the prevailing fashion in England. Ironically this noteworthy repose derived simply from the fact that at first the actors didn't have the experience to act more freely; with superb nonchalance, the director froze them.

Yeats grew to be disillusioned with the Irish theatre, despite such notable successes as Synge's *Playboy of the Western World,* and complained of it burying its ideals in pure realism. His own brand of symbolic drama developed along very different lines, deriving much inspiration from the Japanese Noh plays, introduced to him by Ezra Pound. These later Yeats plays were written to be mimed or chanted to music, and performed on an intimate stage in a drawing room.

Sadly Yeats' mother suffered two strokes in quick succession which rendered her an invalid for the rest of her days. (She did not die until the beginning of 1900.) Home was an unhappy place, which only made Yeats more anxious to be away, but he was still scared of the future. In 1895 he made a move to escape his father's domination and went to share rooms with Arthur Symons. A little later he took the plunge and rented a place of his own in Woburn Buildings, close to Tavistock Square in Bloomsbury. He was to keep this apartment for many years, and it was there in 1901 that he instituted his famous Monday evenings, when he would entertain friends until the early hours of the morning, perhaps in imitation of Mallarmé's Tuesdays. Ezra Pound was to be a regular visitor, as was the Bengali poet Rabindranath Tagore. The poet Yeats must now have considered himself thoroughly established; he even had a mistress.

LATE VICTORIAN CAFE SOCIETY

FARMER BEING EVICTED

III

Searching For an Identity

Yeats' mistress was a charming married lady called Olivia Shakespear (whom he calls Diana Vernon in his *Autobiographies*). Yeats was extremely grateful for the affair, but it was relatively short-lived, for he could not banish all hope of one day possessing Maud Gonne. Until, that is, he learnt in February 1903 that she had married Major John MacBride, a real man of action, and founder of the Irish Brigade which fought alongside the Boer farmers against the British in South Africa. After this tremendous shock, Yeats turned to other lovers for consolation. He took up for a time with the actress Florence Farr and later with a delicious young masseuse called Mabel Dickinson, with whom he had a pregnancy scare.

Yeats suffered acutely the age-old split in human nature between the thinker and the man of action. He tried hard for years to excel as a doer on the public stages of drama and politics. He desperately wanted to be multi-facetted, but it is almost impossible to be a man of action and a great poet. One activity will inevitably take precedence and absorb all the available energy and attention. The contraries end up by being mutually exclusive. Undoubtedly one side of him relished performing for a crowd, whether appealing to a rabble or arguing loftily in a University debate. But the primary impulse for Yeats was elsewhere. In a telling line of his *Autobiographies* he later wrote: 'The self-conquest of the writer who is not a man of action is style.'

Nationalism helped him find his own identity as a poet by forcing him to confront real issues, to deal with real human experiences, not merely myths at twilight. He was also concerned to bring something positive to the great force of nationalism, to bring something out of it which he could evaluate as a real achievement. He recognized the danger of a nationalism not simply fuelled by but expressing itself only through a corrosive hatred of the English. In 1901, with the help of Lady Gregory, the Irish National Theatre Society was founded, with Yeats as President. It operated through the Abbey Theatre, and it achieved solvency by its popular tours to England. The English had never seen anything like it: acting was revolutionized.

But what life-course was the no-longer-so-young man to take? Maud Gonne occupied far too much of the forefront of his mind. If he could not lose himself in action, perhaps he could in abstract thought. He began to examine ways in which he could hammer out a self-protecting philosophy. His father was to write to him impressively: 'You would be a philosopher and are really a poet.' What he really needed were more and different experiences. An opportunity suddenly beckoned, and in November 1904 Yeats left for a lecture tour of the United States, arranged for him by the American patron of Modernism, John Quinn. This trip had a profound influence on Yeats: it widened his horizons, made him aware of the breadth of his potential as well as his actual audience, and generally matured him. A different man returned.

It seems probable that Yeats was in fact finally Maud Gonne's lover in 1908, though for how long or to what extent is uncertain. By this time Maud was separated from her violent and drunken husband. An intimacy with Yeats for a moment bloomed, which must have been some kind of satisfaction for the long-besotted poet. Perhaps it also helped ultimately to free him from the emotional dominance of this powerful woman.

Also in 1908 Ezra Pound arrived in London from America via Venice. He had a high regard for Yeats, considering him to be the best poet writing in English, although perhaps in need of modernization. Pound himself was the living embodiment of Modernism and he strove to convert Yeats. He spent three winters acting as Yeats' secretary (1913-14, 1914-15, and 1915-16) in a small cottage on the edge of the Ashdown Forest in Sussex. They talked about everything, and in the evenings Pound read to Yeats to save the older man's eyes. Pound believed in minimizing abstract thought in poetry, and in making ideas and images concrete. This was of the utmost use to Yeats, who needed to increase the physical focus of his work. It is a tribute to his modesty (or was it that old timidity?), as well as a tribute to the remarkable gifts of Ezra Pound, that Yeats listened so well and learnt.

Pound was a law unto himself. In his role as 'foreign correspondent' of a small magazine called simply *Poetry*, he solicited some poems from Yeats, then had the cheek to alter them before publication without consulting their author. Yeats was rightly incensed, though he came to accept and even welcome the changes. At this time, Dorothy Shakespear, Olivia's daughter and Pound's future wife, was sharing the cottage with the two poets. The young couple nicknamed Yeats 'the Eagle', no doubt because he had a habit in conversation of sailing about loftily before pouncing. There may well have been a contrary element in Yeats which flew high in order to be shot down. Throughout his life people gave him nicknames, doubtless sensing the different parts he projected, the different disguises. But there nearly always seems to be affection in these sobriquets, and recognition of a person out of the ordinary run of things.

SALMON LEAPING

IV

MATURITY

THE BOOK WHICH marks the watershed in Yeats' poetry is *The Green Helmet* (1910) though its successor *Responsibilities: Poems and a Play* (1914), really emphasized and backed up the change. A fitting title, for in this collection we see Yeats assume not just a mature style, but also, indeed, his poetic and mythic responsibilities. He writes of the lives of his fathers and forefathers raised to an heroic level - the history and destiny of his country, Ireland, accorded five star treatment.

All his life Yeats needed symbols, and he latched on to Theosophy and Rosicrucianism because they allowed his supernatural beliefs to assume an order and an identity. When he organized his ideas into a system of his own, he purveyed a simplified version of traditional occult theories. In *A Vision* (on which he spent much of his time between 1917 and 1925) he arrived at the notion that history and human personality could be ordered through the

28 phases of the moon. His beloved gyres (pronounced with a hard 'g'), whirling cones or spirals, represent the self-destroying or self-renewing processes of civilization. The great thing about Yeats' poetry is that you don't actually need to be familiar with the underlying philosophical system - the poetry makes perfect sense on its own terms, in concrete imagery of real power.

By 1917, Yeats was just about desperate to marry. Lady Gregory thought it would be a good thing; she felt it would settle him and keep him out of trouble. For the last time, Yeats proposed to Maud Gonne (her husband had been executed in the Easter Rising of 1916), and when she again refused him, he approached her beautiful young daughter Iseult. But this was not to be either, and thankfully there was a third possibility, in the form of Georgie Hyde-Lees, an English girl first introduced to Yeats in 1911 by Olivia Shakespear. Georgie, 27 years younger than Yeats, accepted his offer and the couple were married in London on 20 October 1917 at the Victorian Registry Office on the Harrow Road. Ezra Pound was best man. Almost immediately Yeats was smitten with remorse: should he have married Iseult or Maud Gonne? Had he made a mistake? But the new marriage was saved when George (as she was now known) attempted automatic writing on the honeymoon, and was rewarded with unlooked-for success. She developed great skills as a medium and Yeats was entranced; it also meant he no longer

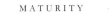

THE MEENAUNE CLIFFS, ACHILL

KILLERY BAY

had to attend seances. The results of him putting questions to her and various spirits writing responses was an enormous inspiration to his late work. It was, in some senses, his raw material.

At the same time, Yeats fell deeply in love with George, and achieved a new kind of serenity and peace. They lived to begin with in Woburn Buildings, and then moved to Oxford for a time. In 1919 they moved into their summer home, a Norman tower near Gort in Galway, which Yeats had bought and they had renovated, called Thoor Ballylee. Just prior to their moving in, a daughter Anne was born, who grew up to be a set designer for the Abbey Theatre and a painter. She was followed by a son, Michael, in August 1921. He became a lawyer, a Senator like his father, and a member of the European government. In addition to love, George brought with her a private income, which was a welcome novelty for the usually strapped-for-cash Yeats.

Back in 1910, Yeats had been granted a government pension which had finally helped to give him a degree of financial security, at the somewhat advanced age of 45. But how did accepting money from the British sit with his nationalist beliefs? It was evidently more important to Yeats that he received this mark of recognition and respect from the Establishment than that he should stir up the political issue. Poetry now was supreme, and the accolade had been to his writing. Yet the contradictions in his nature continue to emerge in his deeds. He may have accepted a pension, but he certainly turned down a knighthood because of his belief in Ireland's independence.

From October 1919 until May 1920 Yeats was in America on another very successful lecture tour, reading and discussing his poetry. George accompanied him and met Yeats' father in New York, with whom she got on famously. It was yet another feather in her cap - she was friendly with everyone. The tour earnt Yeats some money, which was increasingly important now he had a family to support. Yeats had existed for many years on loans and the generosity of others. (From his sisters, from John O'Leary and Lady Gregory.) He had so restricted an actual income that at one point he was even investigated by the Inland Revenue who could scarcely believe that anyone could legitimately live on so little.

In 1922 George decided that the family should be back in Ireland, so she went ahead and bought a house in Merrion Square, the most fashionable address in Dublin. During the 1920s there was something of a reaction against romanticism and nationalism. Perhaps the new spirit was best shown in the figure of the ex-patriot James Joyce. At the same time a threat to the Abbey appeared in Dublin's Gate Theatre, founded by Hilton Edwards and

Micheal MacLiammoir, with an international repertoire and an expressionist leaning. For a moment or two, Yeats may have seemed obscure and out of date, but it is a tribute to both his personal toughness and to the quality of his work that he won through to even greater acclaim within his lifetime.

In 1922 Yeats was offered a seat in the Irish Senate, which he willingly accepted. Dressed in a top hat and frock coat he solemnly attended the afternoon sessions, often saying little. But he made an impression - as always - as a public figure. He particularly distinguished himself in debates on coinage and copyright, and was instrumental in provoking action on both issues. But when he had voted for the creation of an Irish Free State, he quarrelled irreparably with his brother Jack, a staunch Republican. Ireland was divided north and south and in the ensuing bitterness, families were split apart in bloody civil war.

In 1923 Yeats won the Nobel Prize for literature. Aside from the honour, he was chiefly interested in the cash that came with it. He spent some on new furnishings for his Dublin house (including a gilded cage for 50 canaries in his study), but was careful to invest the remainder. In 1925 he published *A Vision*, the most exact statement of his intensely personal philosophy - an idiosyncratic mix of the astrological, the mystical and the historical. It is a key text, but makes strenuous reading.

The Yeatses began to visit the Mediterranean ever more frequently, for the sake of WB's health. They went to Sicily and Capri, and in 1928, with Yeats clearly exhausted, they wound up in Rapallo, where Ezra Pound was living surrounded by a circle of young Modernists. This was to become their favourite resort for the next few years. Yeats' best book of poetry to date, *The Tower,* was published that year, in which he rails at old age and the tragedy of death. He was going deaf, his eyesight was failing, and things could only get worse. In 1929 the family were back in Ireland and made their last visit to Thoor Ballylee; it was too damp for Yeats' lungs. (During the years between 1926 and 1932 he nearly died twice - once of congestion of the lungs, not helped by the fact that he was a smoker. The second time he contracted Malta Fever at Christmas 1929 and was so ill that he made a one-sentence will witnessed by Pound and his young poetic acolyte Basil Bunting, leaving everything to his wife for the use of the children.) Time was running out for Yeats: he knew it and was angry.

THE MEETING OF THE WATER, KILLARNEY

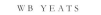

WATERFORD

V

PERSONAL RECOLLECTIONS

THE ONE thing that makes an historical figure spring to life is talking to people who actually knew the person. As the years go on, this becomes increasingly difficult in the case of Yeats, but I have been fortunate enough to know three people, sadly all now dead, who did know him. In the mid 1980s I came to know the Surrealist painter Eileen Agar (1899-1991), and was able to help her write her autobiography *A Look at My Life* (London 1988). During a long life Eileen had met a great many people, from Kipling to Picasso, and from Evelyn Waugh to Ezra Pound. Her second husband was the collector and man of letters Joseph Bard (1892-1975), with whom she met some of the leading literary figures of the Modern Movement. Eileen and Joseph met Pound in Rapallo in 1927 when they were wintering in nearby Portofino, and saw him frequently. Eileen described him as wearing a black corduroy suit which he said was a present from its former owner WB Yeats. Joseph, a great conversationalist, remembered striding along the shore between Pound and Yeats, discussing literary matters. Pound was irreverent. Borrowing Yeats' spectacles he gave them to Joseph to try on, asking him: 'Do you see fairies?'

Was this a typical attitude towards Yeats, or was it just Pound's mischievous nature? In the *Pisan Cantos* Pound calls Yeats 'Old Billyum'. On another occasion, walking again with Yeats and Pound, Joseph heard Pound grumbling, as Eileen put it, 'about the forced continuation of lyrics which sound well enough in a half-lit drawing-room when pronounced by melodious Irishmen, but do not adequately capture the observations and lights of our age.' Pound's obsession was to 'make it new', and he was often intolerant and suspicious of those who didn't match his intellectual template. Like many creative people Pound had a tendency to paranoia.

The other tale about Yeats in Eileen's book dates from this period, 1928. She writes that the only time she heard him laugh was when he recounted the story of how as a Senator, he had received a delegation of Indian revolutionaries. 'They had come to ask for a dozen Irish assassins because the Indians lacked moral courage. Yeats laughed and laughed; the word 'moral' tickled him.' Eileen went on: 'Ezra was often less than kind to Yeats. To Joseph he whispered that Uncle William wrote some fine lyrics in his youth, but had long since lost his way. Yeats seemed slightly afraid of Pound, very much on his guard, and whenever possible, avoided being drawn into discussions on modern poetry. Joseph found Yeats melancholy, sweet and with an inbuilt kindness.'

The artist Robert Medley (1905-1994) was co-founder with the dancer Rupert Doone (1903-66) of the 1930s experimental Group Theatre in which Yeats was interested. Medley had been a student at the Slade School of Art at much the same time as Eileen Agar, and kept in contact with her. When I interviewed him towards the end of his life for the National Sound Archive, he talked less about the Group Theatre than about other periods of his life, feeling that it had been covered fairly thoroughly in several recently published books. In his autobiography, *Drawn from the Life: A Memoir* (London, 1983) Medley makes it clear that he had known Yeats less well that had his partner, Rupert Doone. He does, however, recall one evening when TS Eliot, after much disagreement with Yeats, apparently felt like kicking him downstairs. There was also the occasion when Doone took Yeats for lunch at the Savile Club. Yeats paused to look in the mirror on the stairs and said - to Doone's delight - 'One must always adjust the Image.'

Another old friend of Eileen Agar's, whom I also got to known in the 1980s, was PL Travers (1899-1996), author of the Mary Poppins books. She arrived in England from the Australian bush in the mid-1920s, and immediately set about visiting her Irish relatives back in the old country. While in Dublin she met AE, who had already published one of her poems in his journal, *The Irish Statesman*. It was through AE that Travers met Yeats, of whom she had a beautiful and moving story to recount.

One day, travelling through the countryside back to Dublin, Travers passed near Lough Gill. She remembered that Yeats' *Lake Isle of Innisfree* was actually in the lough, and she determined to visit it, commandeering a boatman for the purpose. After a rough passage, there was no bee-loud glade to be seen, but the island was covered with fruiting rowan trees. She decided to take some branches back to the poet in Dublin as a tribute, and ended up picking a great many. After several mishaps and a storm she reached his home in Merrion Square. Yeats himself opened the door to the soaked girl.

'For an articulate man to be struck dumb is, you can imagine, rare', writes Travers in her excellent volume of essays *What the Bee Knows* (London, 1989). 'But struck dumb he was at the sight of me. In shame, I heard him cry a name into the dark beyond of the house and saw him hurriedly escape upstairs. Then the name came forward in human shape and took me gently, as though I were ill or lost or witless, down to the basement kitchen. There I was warmed and dried and given cocoa; the dreadful branches were taken

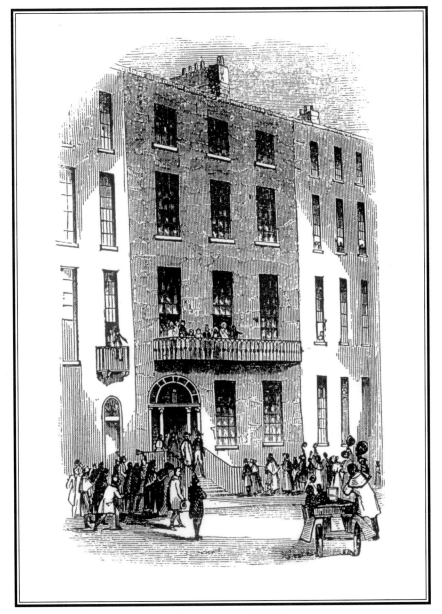

MERRION SQUARE, DUBLIN

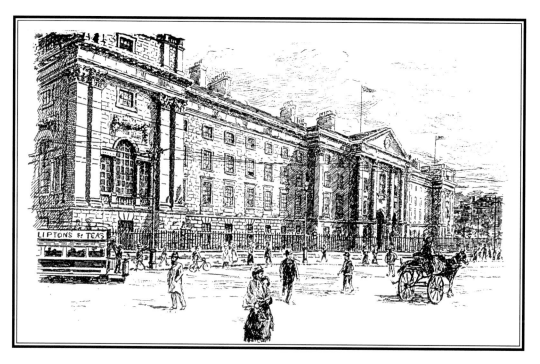

TRINITY COLLEGE, DUBLIN

away. I felt like someone who had died and was now contentedly on the other side, certain that nothing more could happen. In this dreamlike state, I was gathering myself to go - out the back way if possible - never to be seen again. But a maid came bustling kindly in and said - as though to someone still alive! - 'The master will see you now.' I was horrified. This was the last straw. 'What for?' I wanted to know. 'Ah, then, you'll see. He has his ways.'

Yeats greeted her with the news that his canary had laid an egg, then proceeded to show her around the study, 'I getting better every minute and he telling me which of his books he liked and how, when he got an idea for a poem - there was a long momentous pause, here. He was always the bard, always filling the role of poet, not play-acting but knowing well the role's requirements and giving them their due. He never came into a room, he *entered* it; walking around his study was a ceremonial peregrination, wonderful to witness. 'When I get an idea for a poem,' he went on, oracularly, 'I take down one of my own books and read it and then I go on from there.' Moses explaining his tablets couldn't have moved me more. And so, serenely, we came to the end of the pilgrimage and I was just about to bid him goodbye when I noticed on his desk a vase of water and in it one sprig of fruiting rowan. I glanced at him distrustfully. 'Was he teaching me a lesson?' I wondered, for at that age one cannot accept to be taught. But he wasn't; I knew it by the look on his face. He would do nothing so banal. He was not trying to enlighten me and so I was enlightened and found a connection in the process. It needed only a sprig, said the lesson. And I learned, also, something about writing. The secret is to say less than you need. You don't want a forest, a leaf will do.'

AE was Travers' especial friend, who acted as something of a mentor to the aspiring writer. She remembered the younger members of the AE circle calling Yeats affectionately but rather facetiously 'the Flipper', on account of the emphatic theatrical gestures of his right hand. When AE lay dying in the summer of 1935, PL Travers acted as his secretary, informing people, and reading out letters from old friends. It became evident that AE was waiting to hear from Yeats. Travers finally wired to him 'AE dying and daily looking for a word from you.' As she writes, 'It struck home. 'Give my old friend my love', wired Yeats. And with that AE seemed content.' He died that night after making his peace with the world. Yeats came to the funeral in Dublin.

In some kind of summary, PL Travers writes of AE and Yeats: 'They were always willing to concede that there were more things in heaven and earth than philosophy dreamed of. They allowed for the unknown. And, as you can imagine, I took great heart from this.' These different memories show different sides to the man Yeats, and add a personal slant to the poet. They help connect us with the complex reality of William Butler Yeats, and perhaps to understand him a little better.

WATERFORD

VI

LATE FLOWERING AND DEATH

WB YEATS wrote of one of his poems that he 'made it out of a mouthful of air'. This usefully reminds us that literature is made of words and words are merely sounds formed by the passage of air over the vocal organs. Hot air usually, though not necessarily empty chatter. Yeats managed to invest his chosen words with worlds of meaning and emotional resonance, with echoes and connotations as well as with satisfyingly concrete imagery. But the mouthful of air immediately takes us back to the origins of poetry - to the oral tradition and the blind bards who sang or recited the great epics. These long narrative poems were kept alive in men's minds rather than committed safely to paper. They were also, no doubt, polished and subtly reinterpreted from generation to generation, and therefore constituted a living tradition, and one to which Yeats, with his deep interest in folk tales told by the fire, would readily respond.

One of the key facts to remember about Yeats is that despite his sincere nationalism, he wrote in English and not in Irish. English was his chosen language, his medium, his tool, as an artist may use paint as opposed to carving marble. The fact that he wrote in English meant that he not only gained admirers and publishers in the United Kingdom, but that America was open to him as well, a situation which he further turned to his advantage with lucrative lecture tours. Although Yeats was tone deaf, he had an ear for the telling poetic rhyme and rhythm. His poems sound good, even when their content is involved. Yeats used plain speech to evoke a whole range of emotions, and what did it matter if the progression of his thought was occasionally illogical, when it made deep gut sense to the ordinary hearer?

The decade of the 1930s was a period of great change, when events upon the world stage were preparing to convulse the nation states of Europe. Yeats, like so many literary men, flirted with the notion of Fascism, but thankfully did not entertain its ideals too closely. Meanwhile, his greatest patron, friend and comforter, was slowly taking leave of the world. During her last illness, Yeats went to stay at Coole Park with Lady Gregory who had been his support for nearly 40 years. In May 1932 she died. Yeats had once written 'I cannot realize the world without her', but now he had to. It was the end of an era.

THE CLADDAGH

DIGGING UP POTATOES BY THE COAST

In 1934 Yeats underwent the Steinach 'monkey gland' rejuvenating operation, much to his doctor friend Gogarty's disapproval. It was performed by the Australian sexologist Norman Haire. Was it another psychic experiment, or simple vanity? Yeats had raged at growing old; after the operation he was driven even more insistently by rage and renovated lust. He claimed to experience a marvellous renewal of sexual and poetic energy, forces he considered to be closely bound together. Yeats embarked upon a number of late love affairs which his wife countenanced for his sake.

Thus commenced the last pattern of his life, in which Yeats went off on adventures (with Margaret Ruddock, an actress who went mad, with the romantic novelist Ethel Mannin, with Dorothy Wellesley, poet and bisexual Duchess of Wellington), returning to George exhausted and overweight, for rest and relaxation. In the Sussex home of another lover - the journalist Edith Shackleton Heald - Yeats composed some of his last poems. As an old man he wanted more freedom, and his remarkably tolerant wife gave it to him.

As man and poet, Yeats was feudal and agricultural (in manner often verging on the haughty and aristocratic), whereas a writer like Joyce took his subject from the urban and demotic. In many ways Yeats can be said to have invented himself. His external persona was very different from the inner man, and it is no coincidence that he was obsessed with the figurative and literal wearing of masks. He said 'we make poetry out of the quarrel with ourselves', and this certainly applied whole-heartedly to him.

Yeats possessed the gift of conjuring intense verbal magic, of rhetoric (as much in his lectures and speeches as in his more considered writings), and an innate feeling for, and management of, grandiloquence. His authority comes from the rhythm of his words: this was how he spoke, in a majestic, rhythmic, incantatory manner. Above all, what Yeats was able to do was to place his ideas at the service of his poetry, and not let them dominate and overshadow the verse. Ultimately he was dedicated to the life of the imagination, as rooted in real experience, not manifested in abstractions.

There is no whiff in his verse of the midnight oil or the study, though Yeats did in fact work hard at his poems, writing and re-writing them. He aimed at an effect of effortlessness, and it's amazing how regularly he achieved it. He was also prolific. Besides the poetry he wrote many plays and a great deal of prose. There are quantities of reviews and essays to his name besides the famous *Autobiographies*, of which there are several unpublished versions. Yet he seems not to have understood other writers very well - though he was generous in helping the younger generation such as Pound and Joyce - and his selection for *The Oxford Book of Modern Verse* (1936) is still controversial. There are too many minor voices included and none of the great First World War poets such as Wilfred Owen.

JB Priestley identified in Yeats 'a strong personality, increasingly massive with age; unusual self-discipline, enabling him to shape his life as well as his art; and behind the grave and elaborate poet-magician persona he faced the world with, not without an inner gleam of Irish impudence and humour, considerably more common sense than the saints, drunkards, hard-living horsemen he was fond of praising but did not imitate.'

If he was accused in later life of being too aristocratic, it was partly because he had created himself in that mould, an heroic mould, to match the pitch of his feeling for Ireland and the Irish. In this view of things, Maud Gonne was another Helen of Troy. Yeats was also accused of being disdainful. I see this as in part a defence mechanism. He was a man who wished to be myriad-minded. He was ambitious, but not entirely unrealistic. Well, if he could not actually contain multitudes, he could at least project them. Yeats acted many parts, and undoubtedly one of them was the Grand Old Man, who sometimes had a habit of condescending. We must forgive him this, for the sake of his genius.

On 28th January 1939 WB Yeats died of heart failure, aged 73, and was buried temporarily in Roquebrune, the French town where he'd been staying. His remains were brought back to Ireland in 1948, and interred under Ben Bulben in Sligo. According to his wishes, on his gravestone were carved the last three curiously calm, even stoical, lines of his late poem *Under Ben Bulben:*

> Cast a cold eye
>
> On life, on death.
>
> Horseman, pass by!

WB Yeats' early work is very different from the late work, so much so that it might be expected to attract two separate kinds of audience. Yet there is a continuity of mind and of soul throughout the oeuvre, a recognizable flavour, which might switch its manifestation, but not its ultimate identity. A need for sincerity drove him, an honest seeking after poetic and spiritual truth. He was ruthless in his self-investigation, which he pursued relentlessly for the sake of his art, although, like most of us, he was blind to some of his own shortcomings, and could as a result be timid or petty or arrogant. But then the poet didn't have to be consistent: he had a special role to play, a duty to himself and society. As his father once wrote to him:

A DONEGAL HARVEST

CUTTING THE TURF

A poet should feel quite free to say in the morning that he believes in marriage and in the evening that he now no longer believes in it; in the morning that he believes in God and in the evening that he does not believe in God, the important thing being not that he keep his mental consistency but that he preserve the integrity of his soul.

Poetry to Yeats was better than science or philosophy, it was almost religion. It was the pre-eminent form of knowledge.

The late poems represent a poignant flowering of enormous vitality. The 17th century metaphysical poet John Donne, newly rehabilitated to popular taste, was a key influence on their style. And so, of course, was Ezra Pound. But we must not diminish Yeats' own input. He fought through to a spare, brilliantly colloquial lyricism, which was in fact the logical outcome of his belief that poetry should be rooted in the soil.

But just how alive was Yeats to the detail of the natural, external, world? In a letter of 1889 he admits to confusing young pigeons with sparrows. This is not the mistake of a countryman. Perhaps it was the *idea* of Sligo and Galway that Yeats really cared for; not their actuality. Although he writes of natural things, of animals and landscapes, they are seen with the eye of the mind, not studied with a long, hard look. Yeats sees what he expects to see in nature, not what he has observed. He always looks with more profundity at matters of the heart and soul. For him, the really important task lay in recording a passionate life in natural language.

Yeats has been accused of many things - of being careerist or being too preoccupied with money (though these are large issues for most struggling writers) - and in truth he was many things. Witness the number and variety of his nicknames. He was the Eagle, the Flipper, the Founder, Uncle William, Old Billyum. His wife laughingly called her indiscreet husband 'Willie Tell'. For Dubliners, determined at all costs not to be over-impressed, he was 'That fella' and 'Willy the Spooks' and 'The Gland Old Man'. Yet Yeats was not without a sense of self-awareness, which could result in gentle self-mockery. Once in a Rapallo cafe, talking to George Antheil the avant-garde composer and friend of Ezra Pound, Yeats, with a nod to Blake, pretended to see the ghost of his indigestion sitting in a nearby chair.

NEAR RECESS, CONNEMARA

PASS OF KYLEMORE

The story of Yeats' poetic life is one of gathering simplicity - the gradual process of coming to grips with reality and fighting through to an understanding of it through his writing. The poems are not simply some private self-communing, but a loud and joyous bitter-sweet affirmation of the multiplicity of life. In his verse we witness the genuine excitement of the man. He knew, as does every great poet, that any statement he made could only be provisional, that there is no definitive construction to be put upon the world's shifting sands of nuance and meaning. In a late letter he wrote: 'Man can embody the truth but he cannot know it.' He could very well be right.

London: Winter 1999

POEMS

THE LAKE ISLE OF INNISFREE

I WILL arise and go now, and go to Innisfree,
And a small cabin build there, of clay and wattles made:
Nine bean-rows will I have there, a hive for the honey-bee,
And live alone in the bee-loud glade.

And I shall have some peace there, for peace comes dropping slow,
Dropping from the veils of the morning to where the cricket sings;
There midnight's all a glimmer, and noon a purple glow,
And evening full of the linnet's wings.

I will arise and go now, for always night and day
I hear lake water lapping with low sounds by the shore;
While I stand on the roadway, or on the pavements grey,
I hear it in the deep heart's core.

WHEN YOU ARE OLD

WHEN you are old and grey and full of sleep,
And nodding by the fire, take down this book,
And slowly read, and dream of the soft look
Your eyes had once, and of their shadows deep;

How many loved your moments of glad grace,
And loved your beauty with love false or true,
But one man loved the pilgrim soul in you,
And loved the sorrows of your changing face;

And bending down beside the glowing bars,
Murmur, a little sadly, how Love fled
And paced upon the mountains overhead
And hid his face amid a crowd of stars.

SLIEVE LEAGUE (THE MOUNTAIN OF THE FLAGSTONES)

HE HEARS THE CRY OF THE SEDGE

I WANDER by the edge
Of this desolate lake
Where wind cries in the sedge :
Until the axle break
That keeps the stars in their round,
And hands hurl in the deep
The banners of East and West,
And the girdle of light is unbound,
Your breast will not lie by the breast
Of your beloved in sleep.

EASTER 1916

I HAVE met them at close of day
Coming with vivid faces
From counter or desk among grey
Eighteenth-century houses.
I have passed with a nod of the head
Or polite meaningless words,
Or have lingered awhile and said
Polite meaningless words,
And thought before I had done
Of a mocking tale or a gibe
To please a companion
Around the fire at the club,
Being certain that they and I
But lived where motley is worn:
All changed, changed utterly:
A terrible beauty is born.

That woman's days were spent
In ignorant good-will,
Her nights in argument
Until her voice grew shrill.
What voice more sweet than hers
When, young and beautiful,
She rode to harriers?
This man had kept a school
And rode our wingèd horse;
This other his helper and friend
Was coming into his force;
He might have won fame in the end,
So sensitive his nature seemed,
So daring and sweet his thought.
This other man I had dreamed
A drunken, vainglorious lout.

He had done most bitter wrong
To some who are near my heart,
Yet I number him in the song;
He, too, has resigned his part
In the casual comedy;
He, too, has been changed in his turn,
Transformed utterly:
A terrible beauty is born.

Hearts with one purpose alone
Through summer and winter seem
Enchanted to a stone
To trouble the living stream.
The horse that comes from the road,
The rider, the birds that range
From cloud to tumbling cloud,
Minute by minute they change;
A shadow of cloud on the stream
Changes minute by minute;
A horse-hoof slides on the brim,
And a horse plashes within it;
The long-legged moor-hens dive,
And hens to moor-cocks call;
Minute by minute they live:
The stone's in the midst of all.

Too long a sacrifice
Can make a stone of the heart.
O when may it suffice?
That is Heaven's part, our part
To murmur name upon name,
As a mother names her child
When sleep at last has come
On limbs that had run wild.

What is it but nightfall?
No, no, not night but death;
Was it needless death after all?
For England may keep faith
For all that is done and said.
We know their dream; enough
To know they dreamed and are dead;
And what if excess of love
Bewildered them till they died?
I write it out in a verse-
MacDonagh and MacBride
And Connolly and Pearse
Now and in time to be,
Wherever green is worn,
Are changed, changed utterly:
A terrible beauty is born.

THE COLLAR-BONE OF A HARE

WOULD I could cast a sail on the water
Where many a king has gone
And many a king's daughter,
And alight at the comely trees and the lawn,
The playing upon pipes and the dancing,
And learn that the best thing is
To change my loves while dancing
And pay but a kiss for a kiss.

I would find by the edge of that water
The collar-bone of a hare
Worn thin by the lapping of water,
And pierce it through with a gimlet, and stare
At the old bitter world where they marry in churches,
And laugh over the untroubled water
At all who marry in churches,
Through the white thin bone of a hare.

HILL OF HOWTH AND IRELAND'S EYE, DUBLIN

THE SECOND COMING

TURNING and turning in the widening gyre
The falcon cannot hear the falconer;
Things fall apart; the centre cannot hold;
Mere anarchy is loosed upon the world,
The blood-dimmed tide is loosed, and everywhere
The ceremony of innocence is drowned;
The best lack all conviction, while the worst
Are full of passionate intensity.

Surely some revelation is at hand;
Surely the Second Coming is at hand.
The Second Coming! Hardly are those words out
When a vast image out of *Spiritus Mundi*
Troubles my sight: somewhere in sands of the desert
A shape with lion body and the head of a man,
A gaze blank and pitiless as the sun,
Is moving its slow thighs, while all about it
Reel shadows of the indignant desert birds.
The darkness drops again; but now I know
That twenty centuries of stony sleep
Were vexed to nightmare by a rocking cradle,
And what rough beast, its hour come round at last,
Slouches towards Bethlehem to be born?

DEEP-SEA FISHING, KILLERY BAY

SAILING TO BYZANTIUM

I

THAT is no country for old men. The young
In one another's arms, birds in the trees
—Those dying generations—at their song,
The salmon-falls, the mackerel-crowded seas,
Fish, flesh, or fowl, commend all summer long
Whatever is begotten, born, and dies.
Caught in that sensual music all neglect
Monuments of unageing intellect.

II

An aged man is but a paltry thing,
A tattered coat upon a stick, unless
Soul clap its hands and sing, and louder sing
For every tatter in its mortal dress,
Nor is there singing school but studying
Monuments of its own magnificence;
And therefore I have sailed the seas and come
To the holy city of Byzantium.

III

O sages standing in God's holy fire
As in the gold mosaic of a wall,
Come from the holy fire, perne in a gyre,
And be the singing-masters of my soul.
Consume my heart away; sick with desire
And fastened to a dying animal
It knows not what it is; and gather me
Into the artifice of eternity.

IV

Once out of nature I shall never take
My bodily form from any natural thing,
But such a form as Grecian goldsmiths make
Of hammered gold and gold enamelling
To keep a drowsy Emperor awake;
Or set upon a golden bough to sing
To lords and ladies of Byzantium
Of what is past, or passing, or to come.

WATERY SUNSET, LOUGH LEANE, KILLARNEY

IN MEMORY OF EVA GORE-BOOTH
AND CON MARKIEWICZ

THE light of evening, Lissadell,
Great windows open to the south,
Two girls in silk kimonos, both
Beautiful, one a gazelle.
But a raving autumn shears
Blossom from the summer's wreath;
The older is condemned to death,
Pardoned, drags out lonely years
Conspiring among the ignorant.
I know not what the younger dreams–
Some vague Utopia–and she seems,
When withered old and skeleton-gaunt,
An image of such politics.
Many a time I think to seek
One or the other out and speak
Of that old Georgian mansion, mix
Pictures of the mind, recall
That table and the talk of youth,
Two girls in silk kimonos, both
Beautiful, one a gazelle.

Dear shadows, now you know it all,
All the folly of a fight
With a common wrong or right.
The innocent and the beautiful
Have no enemy but time;
Arise and bid me strike a match
And strike another till time catch;
Should the conflagration climb,
Run till all the sages know.
We the great gazebo built,
They convicted us of guilt;
Bid me strike a match and blow.

BYZANTIUM

THE unpurged images of day recede;
The Emperor's drunken soldiery are abed;
Night resonance recedes, night-walkers' song
After great cathedral gong;
A starlit or a moonlit dome disdains
All that man is,
All mere complexities,
The fury and the mire of human veins.

Before me floats an image, man or shade,
Shade more than man, more image than a shade;
For Hades' bobbin bound in mummy-cloth
May unwind the winding path;
A mouth that has no moisture and no breath
Breathless mouths may summon;
I hail the superhuman;
I call it death-in-life and life-in-death.

Miracle, bird or golden handiwork,
More miracle than bird or handiwork,
Planted on the star-lit golden bough,
Can like the cocks of Hades crow,
Or, by the moon embittered, scorn aloud
In glory of changeless metal
Common bird or petal
And all complexities of mire or blood.

At midnight on the Emperor's pavement flit
Flames that no faggot feeds, nor steel has lit,
Nor storm disturbs, flames begotten of flame,
Where blood-begotten spirits come
And all complexities of fury leave,
Dying into a dance,
An agony of trance,
An agony of flame that cannot singe a sleeve.

Astraddle on the dolphin's mire and blood,
Spirit after spirit! The smithies break the flood,
The golden smithies of the Emperor!
Marbles of the dancing floor
Break bitter furies of complexity,
Those images that yet
Fresh images beget,
That dolphin-torn, that gong-tormented sea.

THE MUNICIPAL GALLERY REVISITED

I

Around me the images of thirty years:
An ambush; pilgrims at the water-side;
Casement upon trial, half hidden by the bars,
Guarded; Griffith staring in hysterical pride;
Kevin O'Higgins' countenance that wears
A gentle questioning look that cannot hide
A soul incapable of remorse or rest;
A revolutionary soldier kneeling to be blessed;

II

An Abbot or Archbishop with an upraised hand
Blessing the Tricolour. 'This is not,' I say,
'The dead Ireland of my youth, but an Ireland
The poets have imagined, terrible and gay'.
Before a woman's portrait suddenly I stand,
Beautiful and gentle in her Venetian way.
I met her all but fifty years ago
For twenty minutes in some studio.

III

Heart-smitten with emotion I sink down,
My heart recovering with covered eyes;
Wherever I had looked I had looked upon
My permanent or impermanent images:
Augusta Gregory's son; her sister's son,
Hugh Lane, 'onlie begetter' of all these;
Hazel Lavery living and dying, that tale
As though some ballad-singer had sung it all;

INNISFALLEN

IV

Mancini's portrait of Augusta Gregory,
'Greatest since Rembrandt,' according to John Synge;
A great ebullient portrait certainly;
But where is the brush that could show anything
Of all that pride and that humility?
And I am in despair that time may bring
Approved patterns of women or of men
But not that selfsame excellence again.

V

My mediaeval knees lack health until they bend,
But in that woman, in that household where
Honour had lived so long, all lacking found.
Childless I thought, 'My children may find here
Deep-rooted things,' but never foresaw its end,
And now that end has come I have not wept;
No fox can foul the lair the badger swept–

VI

(An image out of Spenser and the common tongue).
John Synge, I and Augusta Greory, thought
All that we did, all that we said or sang
Must come from contact with the soil, from that
Contact everything Antaeus-like grew strong.
We three alone in modern times had brought
Everything down to that sole test again,
Dream of the noble and the beggar-man.

VII

And here's John Synge himself, that rooted man,
'Forgetting human words,' a grave deep face.
You that would judge me, do not judge alone
This book or that, come to this hallowed place
Where my friends' portraits hang and look thereon;
Ireland's history in their lineaments trace;
Think where man's glory most begins and ends,
And say my glory was I had such friends.

THE CIRCUS ANIMALS' DESERTION

I

I SOUGHT a theme and sought for it in vain,
I sought it daily for six weeks or so.
Maybe at last, being but a broken man,
I must be satisfied with my heart, although
Winter and summer till old age began
My circus animals were all on show,
Those stilted boys, that burnished chariot,
Lion and woman and the Lord knows what.

II

What can I but enumerate old themes?
First that sea-rider Oisin led by the nose
Through three enchanted islands, allegorical dreams,
Vain gaiety, vain battle, vain repose,
Themes of the embittered heart, or so it seems,
That might adorn old songs or courtly shows;
But what cared I that set him on to ride,
I, starved for the bosom of his faery bride?

And then a counter-truth filled out its play,
The Countess Cathleen was the name I gave it;
She, pity-crazed, had given her soul away,
But masterful Heaven had intervened to save it.
I thought my dear must her own soul destroy,
So did fanaticism and hate enslave it,
And this brought forth a dream and soon enough
This dream itself had all my thought and love.

And when the Fool and Blind Man stole the bread
Cuchulain fought the ungovernable sea;
Heart-mysteries there, and yet when all is said
It was the dream itself enchanted me:
Character isolated by a deed
To engross the present and dominate memory.
Players and painted stage took all my love,
And not those things that they were emblems of.

III

Those masterful images because complete
Grew in pure mind, but out of what began?
A mound of refuse or the sweepings of a street,
Old kettles, old bottles, and a broken can,
Old iron, old bones, old rags, that raving slut
Who keeps the till. Now that my ladder's gone,
I must lie down where all the ladders start,
In the foul rag-and-bone shop of the heart.

UNDER BEN BULBEN

I

SWEAR by what the sages spoke
Round the Mareotic Lake
That the Witch of Atlas knew,
Spoke and set the crocks a-crow.

Swear by those horsemen, by those women
Complexion and form prove superhuman,
That pale, long-visaged company
That air in immortality
Completeness of their passions won;
Now they ride the wintry dawn
Where Ben Belben sets the scene.

Here's the gist of what they mean.

II

Many times man lives and dies
Between his two eternities,
That of race and that of soul,
And ancient Ireland knew it all.
Whether man die in his bed
Or the rifle knocks him dead,
A brief parting from those dear
Is the worst man has to fear.
Though grave-diggers' toil is long,
Sharp their spades, their muscles strong,
They but thrust their buried men
Back in the human mind again.

III

You that Mitchel's prayer have heard,
'Send war in our time, O Lord!'
Know that when all words are said
And a man is fighting mad,
Something drops from eyes long blind,
He completes his partial mind,
For an instant stands at ease,
Laughs aloud, his heart at peace.
Even the wisest man grows tense
With some sort of violence
Before he can accomplished fate,
Know his work or choose his mate.

IV

Poet and sculptor, do the work,
Nor let the modish painter shirk
What his great forefathers did,
Bring the soul of man to God,
Make him fill the cradles right.

Measurement began our might:
Forms a stark Egyptian thought,
Forms that gentler Phidias wrought.
Michael Angelo left a proof
On the Sistine Chapel roof,
Where but half-awakened Adam
Can disturb globe-trotting Madam
Till her bowels are in heat,

Proof that there's a purpose set
Before the secret working mind:
Profane perfection of mankind.

Quattrocento put in paint
On backgrounds for a God or Saint
Gardens where a soul's at ease;
Where everything that meets the eye,
Flowers and grass and cloudless sky,
Resemble forms that are or seem
When sleepers wake and yet still dream,
And when it's vanished still declare,
With only bed and bedstead there,
That heavens had opened.
                                        Gyres run on;
When that greater dream had gone
Calvert and Wilson, Blake and Claude,
Prepared a rest for the people of God,
Palmer's phrase, but after that
Confusion fell upon our thought.

                                        v
Irish poets, learn your trade,
Sing whatever is well made,
Scorn the sort now growing up
All out of shape from toe to top,
Their unremembering hearts and heads
Base-born products of base beds.
Sing the peasantry, and then
Hard-riding country gentlemen,

The holiness of monks, and after
Porter-drinkers' randy laughter;
Sing the lords and ladies gay
That were beaten into the clay
Through seven heroic centuries;
Cast your mind on other days
That we in coming days may be
Still the indomitable Irishry.

VI

Under bare Ben Bulben's head
In Drumcliff churchyard Yeats is laid.
An ancestor was rector there
Long years ago, a church stands near,
By the road an ancient cross.
No marble, no conventional phrase;
On limestone quarried near the spot
By his command these words are cut:

> *Cast a cold eye*
> *On life, on death.*
> *Horseman, pass by!*

SAINT COLUMBKILLE'S CROSS

DOWN BY THE SALLEY GARDENS

DOWN by the salley gardens my love and I did meet;
She passed the salley gardens with little snow-white feet.
She bid me take love easy, as the leaves grow on the tree;
But I, being young and foolish, with her would not agree.
In a field by the river my love and I did stand,
And on my leaning shoulder she laid her snow-white hand.
She bid me take life easy, as the grass grows on the weirs;
But I was young and foolish, and now am full of tears.

NEVER GIVE ALL THE HEART

NEVER give all the heart, for love
Will hardly seem worth thinking of
To passionate women if it seem
Certain, and they never dream
That it fades out from kiss to kiss;
For everything that's lovely is
But a brief, dreamy, kind delight.
O never give the heart outright,
For they, for all smooth lips can say,
Have given their hearts up to the play.
And who could play it well enough
If deaf and dumb and blind with love?
He that made this knows all the cost,
For he gave all his heart and lost.

SALMON FISHING, CONNEMARA

WHY SHOULD NOT OLD MEN BE MAD?

WHY should not old men be mad?
Some have known a likely lad
That had a sound fly-fisher's wrist
Turn to a drunken journalist;
A girl that knew all Dante once
Live to bear children to a dunce;
A Helen of social welfare dream,
Climb on a wagonette to scream.
Some think it a matter of course that chance
Should starve good men and bad advance,
That if their neighbours figured plain,
As though upon a lighted screen,
No single story would they find
Of an unbroken happy mind,
A finish worthy of the start.
Young men know nothing of this sort,
Observant old men know it well;
And when they know what old books tell,
And that no better can be had,
Know why an old man should be mad.

A DRUNKEN MAN'S PRAISE OF SOBRIETY

COME swish around, my pretty punk,
And keep me dancing still
That I may stay a sober man
Although I drink my fill.

Sobriety is a jewel
That I do much adore;
And therefore keep me dancing
Though drunkards lie and snore.
O mind your feet, O mind your feet,
Keep dancing like a wave,
And under every dancer
A dead man in his grave.
No ups and downs, my pretty,
A mermaid, not a punk;
A drunkard is a dead man,
And all dead men are drunk.

THE WILD SWANS AT COOLE

THE trees are in their autumn beauty,
The woodland paths are dry,
Under the October twilight the water
Mirrors a still sky;
Upon the brimming water among the stones
Are nine-and-fifty swans.

The nineteenth autumn has come upon me
Since I first made my count;
I saw, before I had well finished,
All suddenly mount
And scatter wheeling in great broken rings
Upon their clamorous wings.

I have looked upon those brilliant creatures,
And now my heart is sore.
All's changed since I, hearing at twilight,
The first time on this shore,
The bell-beat of their wings above my head,
Trod with a lighter tread.

GLENDALOUGH

Unwearied still, lover by lover,
They paddle in the cold
Companionable streams or climb the air;
Their hearts have not grown old;
Passion or conquest, wander where they will,
Attend upon them still.

But now they drift on the still water,
Mysterious, beautiful;
Among what rushes will they build,
By what lake's edge or pool
Delight men's eyes when I awake some day
To find they have flown away?

INDEX OF FIRST LINES

(with each poem's date)

	pages
Around me the images of thirty years (1936-9)	98-101
Come swish around, my pretty punk (1936-9)	114
Down by the salley gardens my love and I did meet (1889)	110
I have met them at close of day (1916)	83-5
I sought a theme and sought for it in vain (1936-9)	102-3
I wander by the edge (1899)	82
I will arise and go now, and go to Innisfree (1893)	78
Never give all the heart, for love (1904)	111
Swear by what the sages spoke (1938)	104-8
That is no country for old men. The young (1927)	91-2
The light of evening, Lissadell (1927)	94
The trees are in their autumn beauty (1919)	116-8
The unpurged images of day recede (1930)	96-7
Turning and turning in the widening gyre (1921)	88
When you are old and grey and full of sleep (1893)	80
Why should not old men be mad? (1936-9)	113
Would I could cast a sail on the water (1919)	86

SELECTED FURTHER READING

The Complete Works of WB Yeats
(especially Collected Poems and Autobiographies)

WB Yeats by Micheal MacLiammoir and Eavan Boland (London, 1971)

Yeats: The Man and the Masks by Richard Ellmann (London, 1979)

WB Yeats: A Life by Stephen Coote (London, 1997)

WB Yeats: The Man and the Milieu by Keith Alldritt (London, 1997)